CHINESE
HOROSCOPES
FOR
LOVERS

The
Ox

LORI REID

illustrated by
PAUL COLLICUTT

ELEMENT BOOKS

Shaftesbury, Dorset • Rockport, Massachusetts • Brisbane, Queensland

© Lori Reid 1996

First published in Great Britain in 1996 by

ELEMENT BOOKS LIMITED

Shaftesbury, Dorset SP7 8BP

Published in the USA in 1996 by

ELEMENT BOOKS, INC.

PO Box 830, Rockport, MA 01966

Published in Australia in 1996 by

ELEMENT BOOKS LIMITED

for JACARANDA WILEY LIMITED

33 Park Road, Milton, Brisbane 4064

Designed and created by

THE BRIDGEWATER BOOK COMPANY

Art directed by *Peter Bridgewater*

Designed by *Angela Neal*

Picture research by *Vanessa Fletcher*

Edited by *Gillian Delaforce*

Printed and bound in Great Britain by
BPC Paulton Books Ltd

British Library Cataloguing in Publication data available

Library of Congress Cataloging in Publication data available

ISBN 1-85230-762-5

Contents

牛

8

*Why are
some people
lucky in
love and
others not?*

Chinese Astrology

SOME PEOPLE fall in love and, as the fairy tales go, live happily ever after. Others fall in love – again and again, make the same mistakes every time and never form a lasting relationship. Most of us come between these two extremes,

and some people form remarkably successful unions while others make spectacular disasters of their personal lives. Why are some people lucky in love while others have the odds stacked against them?

ANIMAL NAMES
According to the philosophy
of the Far East, luck has very
little to do with it. The answer, the philosophers say, lies with 'the Animal that hides in our hearts'. This Animal, of which there are 12, forms part of the complex art of Chinese Astrology. Each year of a 12-year cycle is attributed an Animal sign, whose characteristics are said to influence worldly events as well as the personality and fate of each living thing that comes under its dominion. The 12 Animals run in sequence, beginning with the Rat and followed by the Ox, Tiger, Rabbit, Dragon, Snake, Horse, Sheep, Monkey, Rooster, Dog and last, but not least, the Pig. Being born in the Year of the Ox, for example, is simply a way of describing what you're like, physically and psychologically. And this is quite different from someone who, for instance, is born in the Year of the Snake.

牛

9

*The 12
Animals
of Chinese
Astrology.*

RELATIONSHIPS

These Animal names are merely the tip of the ice-
berg, considering the complexity of the whole subject.
Yet such are the richness and wisdom of Chinese Astrology that
understanding the principles behind the year in which you were
born will give you powerful insights into your own personality.
The system is very specific about which Animals are compatible
and which are antagonistic and this tells us whether our
relationships will be successful. Marriages are made in heaven, so
the saying goes. The heavens, according to Chinese beliefs, can
point the way. The rest is up to us.

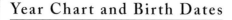

Year Chart and Birth Dates

UNLIKE THE WESTERN CALENDAR, which is based on the Sun, the Oriental year is based on the movement of the Moon, which means that New Year's Day does not fall on a fixed date. This Year Chart, taken from the Chinese Perpetual Calendar, lists the dates on which each year begins and ends together with its Animal ruler for the year. In addition, the Chinese believe that the tangible world is composed of 5 elements, each slightly adapting the characteristics of the Animal signs. These elemental influences are also given here. Finally, the aspect, that is, whether the year is characteristically Yin (-) or Yang (+), is also listed.

The Western calendar is based on the Sun; the Oriental on the Moon.

YIN AND YANG

Yin and Yang are the terms given to the dynamic complementary forces that keep the universe in balance and which are the central principles behind life. Yin is all that is considered negative, passive, feminine, night, the Moon, while Yang is considered positive, active, masculine, day, the Sun.

Year	From – To	Animal sign	Element	Aspect
1900	31 Jan 1900 – 18 Feb 1901	Rat	Metal	+ Yang
1901	19 Feb 1901 – 7 Feb 1902	Ox	Metal	– Yin
1902	8 Feb 1902 – 28 Jan 1903	Tiger	Water	+ Yang
1903	29 Jan 1903 – 15 Feb 1904	Rabbit	Water	– Yin
1904	16 Feb 1904 – 3 Feb 1905	Dragon	Wood	+ Yang
1905	4 Feb 1905 – 24 Jan 1906	Snake	Wood	– Yin
1906	25 Jan 1906 – 12 Feb 1907	Horse	Fire	+ Yang
1907	13 Feb 1907 – 1 Feb 1908	Sheep	Fire	– Yin
1908	2 Feb 1908 – 21 Jan 1909	Monkey	Earth	+ Yang
1909	22 Jan 1909 – 9 Feb 1910	Rooster	Earth	– Yin
1910	10 Feb 1910 – 29 Jan 1911	Dog	Metal	+ Yang
1911	30 Jan 1911 – 17 Feb 1912	Pig	Metal	– Yin
1912	18 Feb 1912 – 5 Feb 1913	Rat	Water	+ Yang
1913	6 Feb 1913 – 25 Jan 1914	Ox	Water	– Yin
1914	26 Jan 1914 – 13 Feb 1915	Tiger	Wood	+ Yang
1915	14 Feb 1915 – 2 Feb 1916	Rabbit	Wood	– Yin
1916	3 Feb 1916 – 22 Jan 1917	Dragon	Fire	+ Yang
1917	23 Jan 1917 – 10 Feb 1918	Snake	Fire	– Yin
1918	11 Feb 1918 – 31 Jan 1919	Horse	Earth	+ Yang
1919	1 Feb 1919 – 19 Feb 1920	Sheep	Earth	– Yin
1920	20 Feb 1920 – 7 Feb 1921	Monkey	Metal	+ Yang
1921	8 Feb 1921 – 27 Jan 1922	Rooster	Metal	– Yin
1922	28 Jan 1922 – 15 Feb 1923	Dog	Water	+ Yang
1923	16 Feb 1923 – 4 Feb 1924	Pig	Water	– Yin
1924	5 Feb 1924 – 24 Jan 1925	Rat	Wood	+ Yang
1925	25 Jan 1925 – 12 Feb 1926	Ox	Wood	– Yin
1926	13 Feb 1926 – 1 Feb 1927	Tiger	Fire	+ Yang
1927	2 Feb 1927 – 22 Jan 1928	Rabbit	Fire	– Yin
1928	23 Jan 1928 – 9 Feb 1929	Dragon	Earth	+ Yang
1929	10 Feb 1929 – 29 Jan 1930	Snake	Earth	– Yin
1930	30 Jan 1930 – 16 Feb 1931	Horse	Metal	+ Yang
1931	17 Feb 1931 – 5 Feb 1932	Sheep	Metal	– Yin
1932	6 Feb 1932 – 25 Jan 1933	Monkey	Water	+ Yang
1933	26 Jan 1933 – 13 Feb 1934	Rooster	Water	– Yin
1934	14 Feb 1934 – 3 Feb 1935	Dog	Wood	+ Yang
1935	4 Feb 1935 – 23 Jan 1936	Pig	Wood	– Yin

Year	From – To	Animal sign	Element	Aspect
1936	24 Jan 1936 – 10 Feb 1937	Rat	Fire	+ Yang
1937	11 Feb 1937 – 30 Jan 1938	Ox	Fire	– Yin
1938	31 Jan 1938 – 18 Feb 1939	Tiger	Earth	+ Yang
1939	19 Feb 1939 – 7 Feb 1940	Rabbit	Earth	– Yin
1940	8 Feb 1940 – 26 Jan 1941	Dragon	Metal	+ Yang
1941	27 Jan 1941 – 14 Feb 1942	Snake	Metal	– Yin
1942	15 Feb 1942 – 4 Feb 1943	Horse	Water	+ Yang
1943	5 Feb 1943 – 24 Jan 1944	Sheep	Water	– Yin
1944	25 Jan 1944 – 12 Feb 1945	Monkey	Wood	+ Yang
1945	13 Feb 1945 – 1 Feb 1946	Rooster	Wood	– Yin
1946	2 Feb 1946 – 21 Jan 1947	Dog	Fire	+ Yang
1947	22 Jan 1947 – 9 Feb 1948	Pig	Fire	– Yin
1948	10 Feb 1948 – 28 Jan 1949	Rat	Earth	+ Yang
1949	29 Jan 1949 – 16 Feb 1950	Ox	Earth	– Yin
1950	17 Feb 1950 – 5 Feb 1951	Tiger	Metal	+ Yang
1951	6 Feb 1951 – 26 Jan 1952	Rabbit	Metal	– Yin
1952	27 Jan 1952 – 13 Feb 1953	Dragon	Water	+ Yang
1953	14 Feb 1953 – 2 Feb 1954	Snake	Water	– Yin
1954	3 Feb 1954 – 23 Jan 1955	Horse	Wood	+ Yang
1955	24 Jan 1955 – 11 Feb 1956	Sheep	Wood	– Yin
1956	12 Feb 1956 – 30 Jan 1957	Monkey	Fire	+ Yang
1957	31 Jan 1957 – 17 Feb 1958	Rooster	Fire	– Yin
1958	18 Feb 1958 – 7 Feb 1959	Dog	Earth	+ Yang
1959	8 Feb 1959 – 27 Jan 1960	Pig	Earth	– Yin
1960	28 Jan 1960 – 14 Feb 1961	Rat	Metal	+ Yang
1961	15 Feb 1961 – 4 Feb 1962	Ox	Metal	– Yin
1962	5 Feb 1962 – 24 Jan 1963	Tiger	Water	+ Yang
1963	25 Jan 1963 – 12 Feb 1964	Rabbit	Water	– Yin
1964	13 Feb 1964 – 1 Feb 1965	Dragon	Wood	+ Yang
1965	2 Feb 1965 – 20 Jan 1966	Snake	Wood	– Yin
1966	21 Jan 1966 – 8 Feb 1967	Horse	Fire	+ Yang
1967	9 Feb 1967 – 29 Jan 1968	Sheep	Fire	– Yin
1968	30 Jan 1968 – 16 Feb 1969	Monkey	Earth	+ Yang
1969	17 Feb 1969 – 5 Feb 1970	Rooster	Earth	– Yin
1970	6 Feb 1970 – 26 Jan 1971	Dog	Metal	+ Yang
1971	27 Jan 1971 – 15 Jan 1972	Pig	Metal	– Yin

Year	From – To	Animal sign	Element	Aspect
1972	16 Jan 1972 – 2 Feb 1973	Rat	Water	+ Yang
1973	3 Feb 1973 – 22 Jan 1974	Ox	Water	– Yin
1974	23 Jan 1974 – 10 Feb 1975	Tiger	Wood	+ Yang
1975	11 Feb 1975 – 30 Jan 1976	Rabbit	Wood	– Yin
1976	31 Jan 1976 – 17 Feb 1977	Dragon	Fire	+ Yang
1977	18 Feb 1977 – 6 Feb 1978	Snake	Fire	– Yin
1978	7 Feb 1978 – 27 Jan 1979	Horse	Earth	+ Yang
1979	28 Jan 1979 – 15 Feb 1980	Sheep	Earth	– Yin
1980	16 Feb 1980 – 4 Feb 1981	Monkey	Metal	+ Yang
1981	5 Feb 1981 – 24 Jan 1982	Rooster	Metal	– Yin
1982	25 Jan 1982 – 12 Feb 1983	Dog	Water	+ Yang
1983	13 Feb 1983 – 1 Feb 1984	Pig	Water	– Yin
1984	2 Feb 1984 – 19 Feb 1985	Rat	Wood	+ Yang
1985	20 Feb 1985 – 8 Feb 1986	Ox	Wood	– Yin
1986	9 Feb 1986 – 28 Jan 1987	Tiger	Fire	+ Yang
1987	29 Jan 1987 – 16 Feb 1988	Rabbit	Fire	– Yin
1988	17 Feb 1988 – 5 Feb 1989	Dragon	Earth	+ Yang
1989	6 Feb 1989 – 26 Jan 1990	Snake	Earth	– Yin
1990	27 Jan 1990 – 14 Feb 1991	Horse	Metal	+ Yang
1991	15 Feb 1991 – 3 Feb 1992	Sheep	Metal	– Yin
1992	4 Feb 1992 – 22 Jan 1993	Monkey	Water	+ Yang
1993	23 Jan 1993 – 9 Feb 1994	Rooster	Water	– Yin
1994	10 Feb 1994 – 30 Jan 1995	Dog	Wood	+ Yang
1995	31 Jan 1995 – 18 Feb 1996	Pig	Wood	– Yin
1996	19 Feb 1996 – 7 Feb 1997	Rat	Fire	+ Yang
1997	8 Feb 1997 – 27 Jan 1998	Ox	Fire	– Yin
1998	28 Jan 1998 – 15 Feb 1999	Tiger	Earth	+ Yang
1999	16 Feb 1999 – 4 Feb 2000	Rabbit	Earth	– Yin
2000	5 Feb 2000 – 23 Jan 2001	Dragon	Metal	+ Yang
2001	24 Jan 2001 – 11 Feb 2002	Snake	Metal	– Yin
2002	12 Feb 2002 – 31 Jan 2003	Horse	Water	+ Yang
2003	1 Feb 2003 – 21 Jan 2004	Sheep	Water	– Yin
2004	22 Jan 2004 – 8 Feb 2005	Monkey	Wood	+ Yang
2005	9 Feb 2005 – 28 Jan 2006	Rooster	Wood	– Yin
2006	29 Jan 2006 – 17 Feb 2007	Dog	Fire	+ Yang
2007	18 Feb 2007 – 6 Feb 2008	Pig	Fire	– Yin

牛

Introducing the Animals

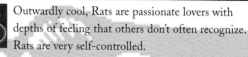

| THE RAT | ♥ ♥ ♥ DRAGON, MONKEY | ✗ HORSE |

 Outwardly cool, Rats are passionate lovers with depths of feeling that others don't often recognize. Rats are very self-controlled.

| THE OX | ♥ ♥ ♥ SNAKE, ROOSTER | ✗ SHEEP |

 Not necessarily the most romantic of the signs, Ox people make steadfast lovers as well as faithful, affectionate partners.

| THE TIGER | ♥ ♥ ♥ HORSE, DOG | ✗ MONKEY |

Passionate and sensual, Tigers are exciting lovers. Flirty when young, once committed they make stable partners and keep their sexual allure.

| THE RABBIT | ♥ ♥ ♥ SHEEP, PIG | ✗ ROOSTER |

Gentle, emotional and sentimental, Rabbits make sensitive lovers. They are shrewd and seek a partner who offers security.

| THE DRAGON | ♥ ♥ ♥ RAT, MONKEY | ✗ DOG |

Dragon folk get as much stimulation from mind-touch as they do through sex. A partner on the same wave-length is essential.

| THE SNAKE | ♥ ♥ ♥ OX, ROOSTER | ✗ PIG |

Deeply passionate, strongly sexed but not aggressive, snakes are attracted to elegant, refined partners. But they are deeply jealous and possessive.

牛

♥ ♥ ♥ *COMPATIBLE* ✖ *INCOMPATIBLE*

THE HORSE	♥ ♥ ♥ TIGER, DOG	✖ RAT

For horse-born folk love is blind. In losing their hearts, they lose their heads and make several mistakes before finding the right partner.

THE SHEEP	♥ ♥ ♥ RABBIT, PIG	✖ OX

Sheep-born people are made for marriage. Domesticated home-lovers, they find emotional satisfaction with a partner who provides security.

THE MONKEY	♥ ♥ ♥ DRAGON, RAT	✖ TIGER

Clever and witty, Monkeys need partners who will keep them stimulated. Forget the 9 to 5 routine, these people need *pizzazz*.

THE ROOSTER	♥ ♥ ♥ OX, SNAKE	✖ RABBIT

The Rooster's stylish good looks guarantee they will attract many suitors. They are level-headed and approach relationships coolly.

THE DOG	♥ ♥ ♥ TIGER, HORSE	✖ DRAGON

A loving, stable relationship is an essential component in the lives of Dogs. Once they have found their mate, they remain faithful for life.

THE PIG	♥ ♥ ♥ RABBIT, SHEEP	✖ SNAKE

These are sensual hedonists who enjoy lingering love-making between satin sheets. Caviar and champagne go down very nicely too.

牛

The Ox Personality

BEING BORN under the influence of the Ox means you're blessed with great endurance and strength of character. Few could match your determination and persistence once you've set your mind on a goal. As the mighty Ox inexorably draws the plough through the soil hour after hour, so you quietly labour at your daily tasks unremittingly and without complaint. You know the way to succeed is by slow sustained effort and you certainly don't believe in get-rich-quick schemes.

OX FACTS

Second in order ★ *Chinese name – Niu* ★ *Sign of industry*
★ *Hour – 1AM-2. 59AM* ★ *Month – January* ★
★ *Western counterpart – Capricorn* ★

CHARACTERISTICS

♥ *Honesty* ♥ *Loyalty* ♥ *Sincerity* ♥ *Steadfastness* ♥ *Integrity*
♥ *Popularity* ♥ *Reliability*

✖ *Stolidity* ✖ *Stubbornness* ✖ *Inflexibility* ✖ *Sulkiness*
✖ *Impatience* ✖ *Narrow-mindedness*

*Ox people are practical and conscientious,
and often work best on their own.*

DOWN-TO-EARTH

Practical, industrious and down-to-earth, you're driven by a
compulsion to work hard and have no truck with free-loaders, nor
with the lazy. Though you have a philosophical turn of mind,
once you've made up your mind over an issue, neither heaven nor
earth can make you change it. This causes accusations of pig-
headedness and inflexibility, but these are the same qualities that
enable you to be staunch and forthright. They contribute
towards your integrity and ability
to shoulder responsibility.

OX AMBITION

It's plain that you're drawn
by the familiar, rather than
by the excitement of the
unknown. But beneath that
unpretentious, placid
exterior of yours lies not
only a heart of gold but
also a clever, determined
mentality, powered by a
driving ambition to succeed.

*Behind the
Ox façade
lies a heart
of gold.*

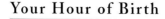

牛

Your Hour of Birth

WHILE YOUR YEAR OF BIRTH describes your fundamental character, the Animal governing the actual hour in which you were born describes your outer temperament, how people see you or the picture you present to the outside world. Note that each Animal rules over two consecutive hours. Also note that these are GMT standard times and that adjustments need to be made if you were born during Summer or daylight saving time.

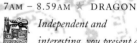

11PM – 12.59AM ★ RAT
Pleasant, sociable, easy to get on with. An active, confident, busy person – and a bit of a busybody to boot.

1AM – 2.59AM ★ OX
Level-headed and down-to-earth, you come across as knowledgeable and reliable – sometimes, though, a bit biased.

3AM – 4.59AM ★ TIGER
Enthusiastic and self-assured, people see you as a strong and positive personality – at times a little over-exuberant.

5AM – 6.59AM ★ RABBIT
You're sensitive and shy and don't project your real self to the world. You feel you have to put on an act to please others.

7AM – 8.59AM ★ DRAGON
Independent and interesting, you present a picture of someone who is quite out of the ordinary.

9AM – 10.59AM ★ SNAKE
You can be a bit difficult to fathom and, because you appear so controlled, people either take to you instantly, or not at all.

牛

19

11AM – 12.59PM ★ HORSE

 Open, cheerful and happy-go-lucky is the picture you always put across to others. You're an extrovert and it generally shows.

1PM – 2.59PM ★ SHEEP

 Your unassuming nature won't allow you to foist yourself upon others so people see you as quiet and retiring – but eminently sensible, though.

3PM – 4.59PM ★ MONKEY

 *Lively and talkative, that twinkle in your eye will guarantee you make friends wherever you go.*

5PM – 6.59PM ★ ROOSTER

 There's something rather stylish in your approach that gives people an impression of elegance and glamour. But you don't suffer fools gladly.

7PM – 8.59PM ★ DOG

Some people see you as steady and reliable, others as quiet and graceful and others still as dull and unimaginative. It all depends who you're with at the time.

9PM – 10.59PM ★ PIG

Your laid-back manner conceals a depth of interest and intelligence that doesn't always come through at first glance.

Your hour of birth describes your outer temperament.

The Ox Lover

In life as well as in love, you tend to be reticent and inward-looking. Cautious and reserved, you keep your feelings to yourself so it takes you a long time to establish a rapport with someone new. Having made friends, you need yet another age before you feel relaxed enough to commit yourself to a serious relationship with this awfully patient partner of yours.

Oxen are reserved and cautious about relationships.

ONE THING ALL OXEN SHARE is a dislike of small-talk. Perhaps this is why you don't enjoy parties much and could probably count all your friends on one hand. You're not really gregarious and would much rather be at home reading a good book. You've been described as dour, a person of few words and this does apply to you in matters of love. Big-hearted you may be, and deeply loving, but verbally demonstrative? Emphatically not!

NO CHANGE

It perhaps takes you so long to make up your mind about choosing a mate because you hate change, so it's essential for you to find someone who is rock-steady in order to make a stable marriage. Apart from an aversion to rushing into things, you're simply not the flirtatious kind. For you, casual affairs and all that romantic kerfuffle simply aren't worth it. So once you're committed you'll probably be faithful and true.

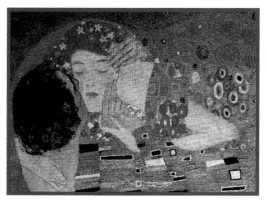

The Kiss
GUSTAV KLIMT 1862-1918

MARRIAGE

Unfortunately, many Ox marriages do fall apart after a few years, possibly because the dominant Ox is too bossy or too inflexible. Or perhaps because, when things go wrong, Oxen tend to blame everyone except themselves. However, if you've been lucky or if you've chosen wisely, you both can build a close-knit family group to which you will devote yourself and which will bring a great deal of happiness into your life.

Ox folk thrive on family life.

In Your Element

ALTHOUGH YOUR SIGN recurs every 12 years, each generation is slightly modified by one of 5 elements. If you were born under the Metal influence your character, emotions and behaviour would show significant variations from an individual born under one of the other elements. Check the Year Chart for your ruling element and discover what effects it has upon you.

THE METAL OX ★ 1901 AND 1961

Being ruled by Metal means that you'll work harder, and more conscientiously, than other Oxen. Your determination and sheer bloody-mindedness won't brook any interference in achieving your aims. You're honest and reliable but your rigidly stiff upper lip makes it difficult for you to show emotion.

THE WATER OX ★ 1913 AND 1973

More flexible than the average Ox type, you're prepared to consider other people's point of view and take their ideas on board, which means you're easy to live with and you generally understand other people's feelings. Patience and integrity, salient characteristics in your nature, ensure your popularity and success.

THE WOOD OX ★ 1925 AND 1985

Tolerant and fair-minded, you're the least obdurate of the Oxen tribe and the most willing to accept change. With a more open attitude towards others, you appreciate the value of co-operative team work and they respect you for your high principles. You're loyal and devoted to those you love.

THE FIRE OX ★ 1937 AND 1997

As a rule Ox folk are not impulsive, but being born under the Fire element gives you dynamic qualities. Your leadership capabilities ensure positions of authority at work and in the community. Though impatient, you're loyal and devoted to your family.

THE EARTH OX ★ 1949

The most reliable and industrious Oxen belong to this group. The Earth element helps you temper many of your negative characteristics. Honest and loyal to your loved ones, you'll toil uncomplainingly to provide them with a secure and comfortable environment.

牛

24

*Rencontre
du Soir
(detail)*
THEOPHILE-
ALEXANDRE
STEINLEN
1859–1923

Partners in Love

THE CHINESE are very definite about which animals are compatible with each other and which are antagonistic. So find out if you're truly suited to your partner.

OX + RAT ★ *Sexually thrilling but disastrous in marriage. Consequently, better as a love affair.*

OX + OX ★ *A good, solid relationship – but where's the pizzazz?*

OX + TIGER ★ *The Chinese say that this is one of the worst matches possible, yet despite the disharmony that's likely to result, you are drawn to each other nevertheless.*

OX + RABBIT ★ *This union promises a contented domestic life. In business you're too laid-back to make a go of it.*

OX + DRAGON ★ *When it comes to stubbornness, you've met your match here and essential give-and-take is lacking.*

OX + SNAKE ★ *Sympathetic, understanding, loving, on the same wave-length – you've got the lot!*

OX + HORSE ★ *Better in business together than in bed.*

OX + SHEEP ★ *Even though your bodies may meet, your minds won't and it's certain your hearts never will.*

OX + MONKEY ★ *When this relationship works, life can be fun, fun, fun.*

Eiaha chipa
PAUL GAUGUIN 1848–1903

LOVE PARTNERS AT A GLANCE		
Ox with:	**Tips on Togetherness**	**Compatibility**
Rat	mutual appreciation	♥♥♥
Ox	solid but stolid	♥♥
Tiger	a clash of temperaments	♥
Rabbit	soft and gentle	♥♥♥
Dragon	first attraction, then dead-lock	♥
Snake	simply sublime	♥♥♥♥
Horse	confrontational	♥
Sheep	in your dreams!	♥
Monkey	a complementary match	♥♥
Rooster	blessed by the gods	♥♥♥♥
Dog	odds against, but a glimmer of hope	♥♥
Pig	worth persisting at	♥♥

COMPATIBILITY RATINGS:
♥ *conflict* ♥♥ *work at it* ♥♥♥ *strong sexual attraction* ♥♥♥♥ *heavenly!*

OX + ROOSTER ★ *Sexy. Passionate. Sizzling. Top marks for a happy and successful relationship.*

OX + DOG ★ *Not much in common between you two and neither is truly comfortable with the other.*

OX + PIG ★ *Plenty of sexual attraction and some shared attitudes can produce harmony.*

Some relationships promise an irresistible magnetism.

牛

26

Hot Dates

IF YOU'RE DATING someone for the first time, taking your partner out for a special occasion or simply wanting to re-ignite that flame of passion between you, it helps to understand what would please that person most.

RATS ★ *Wine and dine him or take her to a party. Do something on impulse… go to the races or take a flight in a hot air balloon.*

OXEN ★ *Go for a drive in the country and drop in on a stately home. Visit an art gallery or antique shops. Then have an intimate dinner à deux.*

'So glad to see you…'
COCA-COLA 1945

TIGERS ★ *Tigers thrive on excitement so go clay-pigeon shooting, Formula One racing or challenge each other to a Quasar dual. A date at the theatre will put stars in your Tiger's eyes.*

RABBITS ★ *Gentle and creative, your Rabbit date will enjoy an evening at home with some take-away food and a romantic video. Play some seductive jazz and snuggle up.*

DRAGONS ★ *Mystery and magic will thrill your Dragon date. Take in a son et lumière show or go to a carnival. Or drive to the coast and sink your toes in the sand as the sun sets.*

SNAKES ★ *Don't do anything too active – these creatures like to take life sloooowly. Hire a row-boat for a long, lazy ride down the river. Give a soothing massage, then glide into a sensual jacuzzi together.*

牛

27

The Carnival
GASTON-DOIN 19/20TH CENTURY

HORSES ★ *Your zany Horse gets easily bored. Take her on a mind-spinning tour of the local attractions. Surprise him with tickets to a musical show. Whatever you do, keep them guessing.*

SHEEP ★ *These folk adore the Arts so visit a museum, gallery or poetry recital. Go to a concert, the ballet, or the opera.*

MONKEYS ★ *The fantastical appeals to this partner, so go to a fancy-dress party or a masked ball, a laser light show or a sci-fi movie.*

ROOSTERS ★ *Grand gestures will impress your Rooster. Escort her to a film première or him to a formal engagement. Dressing up will place this date in seventh heaven.*

DOGS ★ *A cosy dinner will please this most unassuming of partners more than any social occasion. Chatting and story telling will ensure a close understanding.*

PIGS ★ *Arrange a slap-up meal or a lively party, or cruise through the shopping mall. Shopping is one of this partner's favourite hobbies!*

Detail from Chinese Marriage Ceremony
CHINESE PAINTING

Year of Commitment

CAN THE YEAR in which you marry (or make a firm commitment to live together) have any influence upon your marital relationship or the life you and your partner forge together? According to the Orientals, it certainly can. Whether your marriage is fiery, gentle, productive, passionate, insular or sociable doesn't so much depend on your animal nature, as on the nature of the Animal in whose year you tied the knot.

IF YOU MARRY IN A YEAR OF THE…

RAT ★ *your marriage should succeed because ventures starting now attract long-term success. Materially, you won't want and life is full of friendship.*

Marriage Feast
CHINESE PAINTING

OX ★ *your relationship will be solid and tastes conventional. Diligence will be recognized and you'll be well respected.*

TIGER ★ *you'll need plenty of humour to ride out the storms. Marrying in the Year of the Tiger is not auspicious.*

RABBIT ★ *you're wedded under the emblem of lovers. It's auspicious for a happy, carefree relationship, as neither partner wants to rock the boat.*

DRAGON ★ *you're blessed. This year is highly auspicious for luck, happiness and success.*

SNAKE ★ *it's good for romance but sexual entanglements are rife. Your relationship may seem languid, but passions run deep.*

HORSE ★ *chances are you decided to marry on the spur of the moment as the Horse year encourages impetuous behaviour. Marriage now may be volatile.*

SHEEP ★ *your family and home are blessed but watch domestic spending. Money is very easily frittered away.*

Marriage Ceremony
CHINESE PAINTING

MONKEY ★ *married life could be unconventional. As plans go awry your lives could be full of surprises.*

ROOSTER ★ *drama characterizes your married life. Your household will run like clockwork, but bickering could strain your relationship.*

DOG ★ *it's a truly fortunate year and you can expect domestic joy. Prepare for a large family as the Dog is the sign of fertility!*

PIG ★ *it's highly auspicious and there'll be plenty of fun. Watch out for indulgence and excess.*

Marriage Ceremony (detail)
CHINESE PAINTING

Detail from Chinese Marriage Ceremony
CHINESE PAINTING

牛

TYPICAL OX PLEASURES

COLOUR PREFERENCES ★ *Violet*

Moss-agate *Lapis-lazuli* *Jade*

GEMS AND STONES ★ *Jade, emerald, moss-agate, lapis-lazuli*

SUITABLE GIFTS ★ *Tapestry kit, kitchen gadgets, record tokens, cookery or gardening books, slippers, bonsai tree, crossword books*

HOBBIES AND PASTIMES ★ *Marathon running, rugby, body-building, sculpture, gardening, pot-holing, DIY, music, sewing, baking*

HOLIDAY PREFERENCES ★ *Oxen like to stay put so you're happy pottering around at home. And there's always the garden. Whether weeding or sitting in your deck-chair, it's all seventh heaven to you. But if you do get away, you're more likely to go to the mountains, plains or rugged cliffs than Fifth Avenue or the Champs-Elysées.*

Far from the madding crowd...

COUNTRIES LINKED WITH THE OX ★ *Palestine, Syria, Jordan*

The Ox Parent

OXEN MAKE DEEPLY CARING and protective parents, and you'll unselfishly beaver away to provide a stable environment for your precious offspring. In return, you demand that they be courteous, respectful and obedient. Compared to other parents

The family is all-important. you may appear strict, but you're a traditionalist and believe in old-fashioned values. Discipline is important to you and you expect your children to adhere to rules and regulations. For you, rebelliousness is a red rag to a bull.

牛

31

DEVOTION

Many members of your sign have children fairly early on in their lives and then devote themselves totally to their families. As a result, they may find it enormously difficult to cut the apron strings when their young fledgelings eventually fly the nest.

THE OX HABITAT

As an Ox, your home is your castle and retreat – a place of tranquillity for yourself and your loved ones. It may not be a very fashionable house but it will be comfortable. As you're the outdoor type, plants and gardening books will be in evidence. You prefer to live in the country or to have a house with a large garden. Violet is the Ox colour but as this isn't often used in interior design, a combination of dusky pinks and blues are favoured colours. Or else the colour scheme may reflect Nature with gold, moss green and burnt umber. But, since your sign is associated with January, winter colours might be more appropriate.

Animal Babies

FOR SOME parents, their children's personalities harmonize perfectly with their own. Others find that no matter how much they may love their offspring they're just not on the same wavelength. Our children arrive with their characters already well formed and, according to Chinese philosophy, shaped by the influence of their Animal Year. So you should be mindful of the year in which you conceive.

BABIES BORN IN THE YEAR OF THE...

RAT ★ *love being cuddled. They keep on the go – so give them plenty of rest. Later they enjoy collecting things.*

OX ★ *are placid, solid and independent. If not left to their own devices they sulk.*

TIGER ★ *are happy and endearing. As children, they have irrepressible energy. Boys are sporty and girls tom-boys.*

RABBIT ★ *are sensitive and strongly bonded to their mother. They need stability to thrive.*

DRAGON *are independent and imaginative from the start. Encourage any interest that will allow their talents to flourish.*

SNAKE *have great charm. They are slow starters so may need help with school work. Teach them to express feelings.*

One Hundred Children Scroll
ANON, MING PERIOD

HORSE ★ *will burble away contentedly for hours. Talking starts early and they excel in languages.*

SHEEP ★ *are placid, well-behaved and respectful. They are family-oriented and never stray too far from home.*

MONKEY ★ *take an insatiable interest in everything. With agile minds they're quick to learn. They're good-humoured but mischievous!*

ROOSTER ★ *are sociable. Bright and vivacious, their strong adventurous streak best shows itself on a sports field.*

DOG ★ *are cute and cuddly. Easily pleased, they are content just pottering around the house amusing themselves for hours. Common sense is their greatest virtue.*

PIG ★ *are affectionate and friendly. Well-balanced, self-confident children, they're happy-go-lucky and laid-back. They are popular with friends.*

Health, Wealth and Worldly Affairs

BEING BORN INTO THIS SIGN means you have a tendency to become a workaholic, so you must ease up and rest more. Also many of you are in sedentary occupations, so do try to find some time in the day for exercise. You're prone to problems affecting the bones and joints, especially the knees. However, strong and robust, Ox-born folk are, according to ancient wisdom, blessed with long life.

The Manufacture of Porcelain
CHINESE WALLPAPER, QING DYNASTY

CAREER

Capable, honest and conscientious, you toil single-mindedly at your task. Colleagues will marvel at your methodical approach and rely on your high standards. You enjoy routine and are efficient and well organized, and particularly suited to many occupations which allow you to specialize. You prefer large corporations as they offer the security you require, but you work best on your own, since Oxen can be rigid in their views.

Few people are able to put as much consistent effort into their work as you do. And fewer still could discipline themselves to sustain your pace or to work so steadily at the same routine.

OXEN MAKE EXCELLENT:

Painters ✴ Decorators ✴ Carpenters ✴ Mechanics
✴ Farmers ✴ Horticulturists ✴ Engineers ✴ Miners ✴
Draughtsmen ✴ Architects ✴ Army officers ✴ Managers
✴ Quarry workers ✴ Academics ✴ Archaeologists ✴
Orthopaedists ✴ Osteopaths ✴ Physiotherapists
✴ Bankers ✴ Investment brokers ✴ Estate agents ✴

FINANCES

Because you believe in security, you're unlikely to take any wild risks where money is concerned. You're careful in your spending habits. Hard work and a fairly simple lifestyle ensure that you accumulate money steadily, which you then invest wisely, if conservatively, to cushion your old age.

You're happiest in a position behind the scenes or where you're actually in charge. Being an Ox, it's likely that you will be, sooner or later, since your industry and ambition guarantee a rise through the ranks to a position of authority.

FRIENDSHIPS

Oxen are not the most gregarious of creatures and you tend not to mix happily in social gatherings but prefer your privacy and a certain anonymity. You also prefer a few close friends to a large network of acquaintances. Family members provide all the companionship you need.

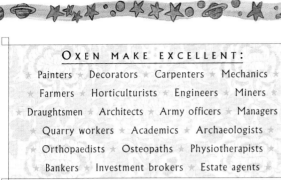

牛

36

East Meets West

COMBINE YOUR Oriental Animal sign with your Western Zodiac birth sign to form a deeper and richer understanding of your character and personality.

ARIES OX
★ With this mix you must be bold and fearless, and you charge through life to reach your goal. In love, you're dominant. A partner who's strong, honest and practical is ideal.

TAUREAN OX
★ You're the most laid-back of the Ox tribe. Diligent and methodical, you get what – and who! – you want in the end. You're sensual with a strong sex drive and a fondness for comfort.

GEMINI OX
★ The Gemini influence adds spirit and vision to your Ox character. Reaching people's minds is more important to you than reaching their hearts. Sex you enjoy, but think romance is strictly for the birds.

CANCERIAN OX
★ Talent, tempered by sensitivity and honed by determination, ensures that you'll develop creative skills to a high degree. Your partner and family are central to your happiness.

LEONINE OX
★ You're a born leader, compelled to take charge of every situation. Sexually ardent, you're a generous lover and happiest with an adoring partner at your side.

VIRGO OX
★ You sometimes fuss over details, but this critical eye helps you choose a mate. He or she will have to meet exacting standards. Not the sexiest of Oxen, with the right partner you'll certainly be the most faithful.

LIBRAN OX
★ Blessed with bags of charm, you're popular and make friends easily. You're peace-loving and never rock the boat, although you do tend to attract those who rock it for you! A born idealist, you're constantly looking for perfection.

 CAPRICORN OX
★ Resolute and implacable, once you've made up your mind you'll steer your ship in your chosen direction regardless. Conservative and responsible, you'll work your socks off to provide security and comfort for your loved ones.

 SCORPIO OX
★ You're very focused: drive, determination and logic characterize your approach in life. In love, you're passionate but hide your emotions beneath a calm exterior. You're a lusty lover so you need to team up with a mate whose libido is as healthy as yours.

 AQUARIAN OX
★ Oxen by nature are solid and predictable. Not you. You're much lighter of spirit and won't lose much sleep if you haven't crossed the t's or dotted the i's. Cool and intelligent, you have a low-boredom threshold, which means you like variety.

 SAGITTARIAN OX
★ Couple your far-sightedness with your tenacity and you'll understand why the world is your oyster. You're born lucky but you're prone to taking the odd shrewd risk. You choose your mate in the same way and, once committed, remain constant.

 PISCEAN OX
★ Sensitivity and introspection temper the characteristic Oxen toughness. You have creative talent and a perspicacity that enables you to get right to the heart of the matter. Romantic and sentimental, it's not so much a partner, more a soul-mate that you seek.

FAMOUS OXEN

Renoir

The Princess of Wales   *Napoleon Bonaparte*   *Adolf Hitler*

Charlie Chaplin   *Marlene Dietrich*   *Paul Newman and Robert Redford*

*The Princess of Wales ★ Dustin Hoffman ★ Twiggy
Paul Newman ★ Robert Redford ★ Bach
Vanessa Redgrave ★ Renoir ★ Fatima Whitbread
Jane Fonda ★ Barbara Cartland ★ Bill Cosby
Richard Gere ★ Mark Knopfler ★ Walt Disney
Bruce Springsteen ★ Napoleon ★ Adolf Hitler
Gershwin ★ Rubens ★ Clark Gable
Charlie Chaplin ★ Marlene Dietrich*

Walt Disney

The Ox Year in Focus

OXEN YEARS BRING STABILITY and measured growth when patient and diligent work pay off. And because of its association with the cultivation of the land, in the Year of the Ox we reap what we have sown and harvest the fruits of past efforts.

HARVEST

Keep a weather-eye on your interests in an Ox Year. Putting decisions on hold in business or affairs of the heart may result in agreements and engagements being cut short or protracted indefinitely. So get your affairs signed, sealed and delivered on the dot this year.

THE DEVIL YOU KNOW

Conservative by nature, this is not a time for grandiose schemes or outrageous fashions. It is a year that favours traditional values and tastes. 'Slow but sure' and 'Better the devil you know' are the mottoes of the Ox.

ACTIVITIES ASSOCIATED
WITH THE YEAR OF THE OX

The discovery, invention, patenting, marketing or manufacturing of: adrenaline, bicycle gears, the hearing aid, chlorophyll, nylon, Fish Fingers, jet engines, the assembly line, crossword puzzles.

牛

40

Your Ox Fortunes
for the Next 12 Years

1996 MARKS THE BEGINNING of a new 12-year cycle in the Chinese calendar. How your relationships and worldly prospects fare will depend on the influence of each Animal year in turn.

1996 YEAR OF THE RAT *19 Feb 1996 – 6 Feb 1997*

In business and financial matters, Oxen do very well in a Rat Year. There could be promotion at work as a reward for previous efforts, or expansion if you're the boss. In matters of the heart it's different – love and lovers go awry.

YEAR TREND: BEWARE RELATIONSHIPS

1997 YEAR OF THE OX *7 Feb 1997 – 27 Jan 1998*

This is your own year so you're quite at home with the steady pace of 1997 and happy to work away in the background making gradual progress. Family life and romance are starred for success.

YEAR TREND: SATISFYING

1998 YEAR OF THE TIGER *28 Jan 1998 – 15 Feb 1999*

The Tiger Year is never an easy time for you with so much drama and tension in the air. Friction at home and at work will have you locking horns frequently with others. Luckily, you're able to keep your head and your perseverance will see you through.

YEAR TREND: A TIME FOR KEEPING YOUR COOL

1999 YEAR OF THE RABBIT *16 Feb 1999 – 4 Feb 2000*

After the drama of the Tiger Year, 1999 is healing. A few wrinkles may have to be ironed out but you can expect success all round, especially in your emotional life. Fortune will smile on relationships.

YEAR TREND: LUCKY IN LOVE

2000 YEAR OF THE DRAGON *5 Feb 2000 – 23 Jan 2001*

Dragon Years favour the daring and the flamboyant, so this is likely to be a frustrating time for you. Your efforts fail to receive the merit they deserve, but you will be kept busy with the changes that escort in the new millennium, and friends will lend a hand.

YEAR TREND: UNPROMISING

The pace accelerates as the year 2000 arrives.

2001 YEAR OF THE SNAKE *24 Jan 2001 – 11 Feb 2002*

Chickens come home to roost this year – which is only fair. Past efforts pay off handsomely and you can take major strides forward. Grab the opportunities offered to you, including invitations that will widen your social network. Romance blossoms.

YEAR TREND: DEEPLY REWARDING

牛

2002 YEAR OF THE HORSE *12 Feb 2002 – 31 Jan 2003*

Events are likely to be volatile – which is not conducive to your temperament. There are likely to be disappointments as life throws the unexpected in your path and affairs of the heart will be fickle.

YEAR TREND: UNSETTLING

2003 YEAR OF THE SHEEP *1 Feb 2003 – 21 Jan 2004*

This year it's a question of swings and roundabouts: what you lose in terms of work and money, you gain in love and romance. Don't take any risks, especially with finances. Focus your attention rather than scattering your energies. Family, friends and lovers bring TLC.

YEAR TREND: EMOTIONALLY UPLIFTING

2004 YEAR OF THE MONKEY *22 Jan 2004 – 8 Feb 2005*

Nothing should be taken for granted in a Monkey Year, so Ox folk might find the going rather trying. And yet honours and recognition could await you as the more wayward aspects of the year defer to your common sense. Romance ticks over.

YEAR TREND: UNEXPECTED OPPORTUNITIES

*Seize the
opportunities
as they occur.*

2005 YEAR OF THE ROOSTER *9 Feb 2005 – 28 Jan 2006*

If life has been in the doldrums over the last few years, take heart. The Rooster Year offers you chances to turn over a new leaf. This may involve a new relationship, a change of job or a major move, and the only proviso is: read the small print carefully.

YEAR TREND: UPWARDLY MOBILE

2006 YEAR OF THE DOG *29 Jan 2006 – 17 Feb 2007*

Other Animals may find Dog Years stressful but Oxen just bulldoze their way through obstacles in their path. Looking back you'll wonder what the fuss was about. This is an excellent year to get married.

YEAR TREND: A PLEASING OUTCOME

2007 YEAR OF THE PIG *18 Feb 2007 – 6 Feb 2008*

The good auspices of 2007 favour those born in the Year of the Ox. You may not make great progress, and financially you should expect modest gains, but life will be stable with the emphasis on revitalization. Relationships and family ties bring amusement and joy.

YEAR TREND: FAVOURS HEARTH AND HOME

PICTURE CREDITS

AKG Berlin/Erich Lessing: pp.24L,
    38 (Napoleon)
AKG London: pp.21, 24B, 26, 27B
e. t. archive: p.34; British Museum: 33T;
    Victoria & Albert Museum: 28, 29
Fine Art Photographic Library Ltd:
    pp.25, 27T, 32-3
Hulton Deutsch Collection: p.38 (all
    except Napoleon and Newman/
    Redford)
Images Colour Library: pp.8, 22T & B,
    23, 30
Kobal Collection: p.38 (Newman/
    Redford)